65/1986L

Holy Night of Miracles

A cantata of hope for Christmas

Lloyd Larson

Companion Products

65/1987L	SAB Score
99/2178L	Performance CD
99/2179L	Bulk Performance CDs (10 pak)
99/2180L	Accompaniment CD
99/2181L	SA/TB Part-dominant Rehearsal CDs (reproducible)
30/2261L	Orchestral Score and Parts
	2 Fl., Ob., 2 Clar., Bsn., 2 F Horns, 3 Tpts., 2 Tbns., Tuba, Timp., Perc., Harp, Pno., Vln. 1 & 2, Vla., Cello, Bass
65/1988L	Performance CD/SATB Score Combination

Editor: Lloyd Larson
Music Engraving: Jeanette Dotson
Cover Design: Jeff Richards

ISBN: 978-0-89328-730-6

© 2007 The Lorenz Publishing Company, a division of The Lorenz Corporation.
All rights reserved. Printed in the U.S.A. Reproduction of this publication
without permission of the publisher is a criminal offense subject to prosecution.

Lorenz Publishing Company
Box 802 · Dayton, Ohio 45401
www.lorenz.com

Foreword

One miraculous night in Bethlehem changed the course of human history forever. Foretold by Old Testament prophets, the Messiah entered the world and, even more importantly, the hearts of people from all walks of life with a message of hope and love. He did not come as many had anticipated—a warrior with strength and force to conquer his adversaries. In the Creator's providential wisdom and timing, a baby came to earth as God in human form. This holy night, the night of Jesus' birth, is recalled annually in our churches and homes as we celebrate the sights, sounds and spirit of Christmas.

Holy Night of Miracles is a reminder that the hope born on that first Christmas night is still needed today and ultimately found in the miraculous Child born in Bethlehem so many years ago. In the timeless message of Christmas, our hearts are touched and renewed with the spirit of Christ's love. It is our prayer that this message and the confident assurance that His birth brought to a small corner of the globe will permeate your life in a fresh way. And may you realize anew the powerful promise that one of God's greatest gifts, represented in this Holy Child, is that of hope—hope for today, tomorrow and for all eternity!

—Lloyd Larson and Niel Lorenz

Contents

O Come to Us, Emmanuel 3
Narration 1 8
Come to Us, O God of Hope 9
Narration 2 16
Do Not Be Afraid 17
Narration 3 26
A Miracle This Holy Night 26
Narration 4 33
Christ Is Born, Sing Glory to God! 33
Narration 5 41
I Was Touched and I Believe 41
Narration 6 51
Child of Hope 51
Narration 7 58
Worship Christ, the Newborn King! 59
Full Narration 71

O Come to Us, Emmanuel

Latin hymn, 9th c.; tr. John M. Neale,
Henry S. Coffin, adapted

Lloyd Larson

O come to us, Em - man - u - el, and

ran - som cap - tive Is - ra - el, that mourns in lone - ly

© 2007 Lorenz Publishing Company, a division of The Lorenz Corporation. All rights reserved. Printed in U.S.A.
Reproduction of this publication without permission of the publisher is a criminal offense subject to prosecution.
THE CCLI LICENSE DOES NOT GRANT PERMISSION TO PHOTOCOPY THIS MUSIC.
www.lorenz.com

JD

ex - ile here un - til the Son of God ap - pear. O

come, thou Rod___ of Jes-se, free thine own from Sa - tan's tyr-an-

ny; from depths of hell thy peo - ple save and

give them vic - t'ry o'er the grave.

Narrator: The prophets said to all who had been made captive, "call upon the Lord, for He has plans to prosper you and give you peace and hope." So the people waited and watched; they prayed for a miracle. Time passed and the days became years. They were dark and very long. The people cried, "O, Messiah, where are You? Where is the promised Warrior, the Conqueror, our Savior, our King? When will He come who shall slay our enemies and lead us to the promised land? We long for a miracle! Come to us, O God of Hope!"

Come to Us, O God of Hope

Niel Lorenz

Lloyd Larson

© 2007 Lorenz Publishing Company, a division of The Lorenz Corporation. All rights reserved. Printed in U.S.A.
Reproduction of this publication without permission of the publisher is a criminal offense subject to prosecution.
THE CCLI LICENSE DOES NOT GRANT PERMISSION TO PHOTOCOPY THIS MUSIC.

www.lorenz.com

JD

high the cost. Come to us, O God of hope, lead us to the

end of night. Give us signs of days fore-told when our dark - ness shall

turn___ to light.___

We long for prom-ised days of peace and, from this e - vil,

Gath - er us in Your em - brace; pro - tect us in e -

seek re-lease.

ter - nal grace. Come to us, O God of hope, lead us to the

14

we'll be led. Come, Mes - si - ah, be our guide; we

we'll be led. Come, Mes - si -

know the Lord is by our side. Come to us, O

ah; the Lord is by our side.

God of hope, lead us to the end of night.

Narrator: And still there was silence and darkness as the people of Israel waited. Generation followed generation as the people of God languished and waited, ruled by darkness and evil. *(pause)* Finally, in the fullness of time, there was in the city of Nazareth, a virgin named Mary who was betrothed to Joseph. An angel of the Lord appeared to Mary and said, "Be not afraid! Rejoice, for the Lord has found favor in you. The Holy Spirit shall come upon you and you shall bear a son and His name shall be called Jesus." *(music begins)* Mary was at first afraid of the meaning of Gabriel's words. But then she answered, "Let it be to me according to your word. My soul magnifies the Lord and I am not afraid. Joseph was also visited by an angel of the Lord and heard the assurance that this was indeed God's plan. So he took Mary as his wife and held her in his heart. He too said, "I trust in the Lord and I am not afraid."

Do Not Be Afraid

Niel Lorenz,
Lloyd Larson

Lloyd Larson

© 2007 Lorenz Publishing Company, a division of The Lorenz Corporation. All rights reserved. Printed in U.S.A.
Reproduction of this publication without permission of the publisher is a criminal offense subject to prosecution.
THE CCLI LICENSE DOES NOT GRANT PERMISSION TO PHOTOCOPY THIS MUSIC.

18

Solo 1 *(Sing 1st time only)*

Ho - ly Spir - it shall come up - on you.

Solo 2 *(Sing 2nd time only)*

fraid! I shall re - joice for I've

Bless - ed be the word of the Lord.

heard the word of the Lord.

Fear not! The child of your womb is the

I am not a - fraid! The

19

Sav - ior. O hear the word of the

child I bear is the prom - ised One of the

1X **2X**
17 18

Lord. Trust the word of the

Lord. I will trust in the

1.　　　　　　　　2.

Lord.
Solo 2 (Mary)
mf

I am not a - Lord.

20

Solo 3 (Joseph)

I shall not fear for the child Ma-ry bears is the Prom-ised One, the

Ho - ly Son of the Lord. I shall not fear for the

an - gel of God has pro - claimed this as the sov - reign will of the

Lord. I'll place my trust in the Lord.

22

A Miracle This Holy Night

Niel Lorenz and
Joseph Mohr

Lloyd Larson
Quoting STILLE NACHT
by Franz Gruber

Narrator: Thus it was that when Mary was great with child, she and Joseph traveled to Bethlehem, to be counted in a census as ordered by the Roman Emperor. While there, Mary gave birth to a Son, wrapped Him in swaddling clothes, and laid Him in a manger, as there was no room for them at the inn. It became clear to all who saw Him that this tiny sleeping Child was the Son of God, the Savior, the promised King. This Child was God's messenger of love, peace and hope to the cold and silent earth. There, in the humblest of places, surrounded by simple shepherds and lowly creatures, Mary took the baby Jesus in her tender arms and whispered, "A miracle is born this holy night. A miracle is born this holy night."

© 2007 Lorenz Publishing Company, a division of The Lorenz Corporation. All rights reserved. Printed in U.S.A.
Reproduction of this publication without permission of the publisher is a criminal offense subject to prosecution.
THE CCLI LICENSE DOES NOT GRANT PERMISSION TO PHOTOCOPY THIS MUSIC.

www.lorenz.com
JD

28

Hold-ing Him in ten-der care a - mid the low - ly crea-tures there, Ma - ry whis-pers at the sight, "A mir - a - cle is born to - night." O ti - ny Child,

Ma - ry whis - pers at the sight,

53
27
p
Si - lent night!
p
Si - lent night! Ho - ly
p
58
28
Ho - ly night! All is calm, all is bright! O
night! All is calm, all is bright!
63
mf
ti-ny Child, born this night; O ho-ly Child, love's pure light; a
mf

mir - a - cle,   this   ho - ly night;   God's mir - a - cle,   born this   ho - ly

night._____

Sleep___   in   heav - en - ly   peace._____

Christ Is Born, Sing Glory to God!

Lloyd Larson and
Traditional French carol

Lloyd Larson
Quoting GLORIA
Traditional French melody

Narrator: And so it had come to pass that on this holiest of nights, this night of miracles, Christ the Savior was born! The heavens rang with angelic sounds and the light of the power and glory of God shone all around. The angels sang, "Glory to God in the highest and on earth, peace and goodwill to all! Christ is born! Christ is born, sing glory to God!"

© 2007 Lorenz Publishing Company, a division of The Lorenz Corporation. All rights reserved. Printed in U.S.A.
Reproduction of this publication without permission of the publisher is a criminal offense subject to prosecution.
THE CCLI LICENSE DOES NOT GRANT PERMISSION TO PHOTOCOPY THIS MUSIC.

34

65/1986L-34

filled with heav-en's light. An an-gel of the

Lord ap - peared and pro-claimed good news for all to hear!_____

Christ is born, sing glo-ry to God in the

Christ is born, sing

cresc.

cresc.

f *mf*

mf

f *mf*

"This shall be a sign," the an - gel said, "you will find the Child in a man - ger bed. Go, wor - ship Christ, the new - born King. Let the heav'ns and earth re -

38

I Was Touched and I Believe

Niel Lorenz

Lloyd Larson

Narrator: Word of Jesus' birth quickly spread and the people praised God for all that was told to them. Angels had brought good tidings of great joy to those waiting in darkness. Those who had persevered with faith in their hearts and believed in the promise were touched by God's gracious love. People everywhere fell to their knees, praising God and saying, "I have heard His word and I trust in the Lord. I have heard the truth. I have been touched by God and I believe."

© 2007 Lorenz Publishing Company, a division of The Lorenz Corporation. All rights reserved. Printed in U.S.A.
Reproduction of this publication without permission of the publisher is a criminal offense subject to prosecution.
THE CCLI LICENSE DOES NOT GRANT PERMISSION TO PHOTOCOPY THIS MUSIC.

44

Lyrics:
I be-lieve.

God in glo-ry came to earth, a prom-ise kept in
mel.

Je-sus' birth. His words of peace all doubts re-lease. I was touched and I be-

46

65/1986L-46

touched and I be - lieve,_____ I be-

lieve._____ My heart was heav-y with the years of

wait - ing, hopes and tears. But then I heard God's ho - ly

48

Child of Hope

Niel Lorenz and
Phillips Brooks

Lloyd Larson
Quoting ST. LOUIS
by Lewis H. Redner

Narrator: *(music begins)* It all began that single miraculous holy night, over two thousand years ago, in the little town of Bethlehem. It began with a promise – a promise made to a people that one day they would be saved. Instead of being saved by a fierce warrior leading a strong army, they – and we – were saved by a tiny Child; a Child of miracles, a Child of everlasting light. Through faith in Jesus, our fears are placed upon His shoulders and He grants us His peace. Through faith in Him, He takes away our sins and gives us His love. This Child is God's promise fulfilled. Through faith in Him, we receive one of God's greatest miracles: the gift of hope.

© 2007 Lorenz Publishing Company, a division of The Lorenz Corporation. All rights reserved. Printed in U.S.A.
Reproduction of this publication without permission of the publisher is a criminal offense subject to prosecution.
THE CCLI LICENSE DOES NOT GRANT PERMISSION TO PHOTOCOPY THIS MUSIC.

52

65/1986L-52

53

54

ho - ly night! Our hopes and fears through all the years are

met in You___ to - night.

Child of hope, You touch my heart with a mes - sage

O Child of hope, You touch my heart, with sim-ple mes - sage

56

Re-new our faith, help us be-lieve. Great gift of God we now re-

ceive. O— Child of ev - er - last - ing light! O

mir - a - cle this ho - ly night! Our hopes and fears through

57

Narrator: This day we celebrate that first holy night of miracles. We give thanks to God for sending His only Son to earth to save us. Let us rededicate ourselves to the God of hope and, like shepherds on that first Christmas night, let us renew our commitment to tell the world of the miracle of Jesus' birth. Christ was born to save us. His message is still one of hope and love. Rejoice and tell the world that the miracle lives on. Christ has come for all! Come. Let us worship Christ, the newborn King!

Worship Christ, the Newborn King!

Lloyd Larson
Quoting familiar hymns

*Angels from the Realms of Glory, *Tune:* REGENT SQUARE *(Henry T. Smart); *Text:* James Montgomery

© 2007 Lorenz Publishing Company, a division of The Lorenz Corporation. All rights reserved. Printed in U.S.A.
Reproduction of this publication without permission of the publisher is a criminal offense subject to prosecution.
THE CCLI LICENSE DOES NOT GRANT PERMISSION TO PHOTOCOPY THIS MUSIC.

60

*Hark! the Herald Angels Sing, *Tune:* MENDELSSOHN *(Felix Mendelssohn); Text:* Charles Wesley

65/1986L-60

61

65/1986L-61

62

Hail the heaven - born Prince of Peace!___ Hail the Sun of
Right - eous - ness! Light and life to all He brings,___
risen with__ heal - ing in His wings. Mild He lays His

glo - ry by,___ born that we no more may die,___ born to raise us from the earth, born to__ give us sec - ond birth. Hark! the her - ald an - gels sing,___ "Glo - ry__ to the new - born__ King."

*O Come, All Ye Faithful, *Tune:* ADESTE FIDELES *(John F. Wade's *Cantus Diversi); Text:* Latin hymn, attr. John F. Wade; tr. Frederick Oakeley

66

65/1986L-66

come, let us a - dore___ Him,___ Christ,___ the

Lord.

Sing, choirs of an - gels, sing____ in ex - ul - ta - tion,

Sing, choirs of an - gels, sing in ex - ul - ta - tion,

sing, all ye cit - i - zens of heaven____ a - bove!

sing, all ye cit - i - zens of heaven____ a - bove!

Glo - ry____ to God, all glo - ry in the high - est.

Glo - ry____ to God, all glo - ry in the high - est. O

Holy Night of Miracles
Narration

O Come to Us, Emmanuel

The prophets said to all who had been made captive, "call upon the Lord, for He has plans to prosper you and give you peace and hope." So the people waited and watched; they prayed for a miracle. Time passed and the days became years. They were dark and very long. The people cried, "O, Messiah, where are You? Where is the promised Warrior, the Conqueror, our Savior, our King? When will He come who shall slay our enemies and lead us to the promised land? We long for a miracle! Come to us, O God of Hope!"

Come to Us, O God of Hope

And still there was silence and darkness as the people of Israel waited. Generation followed generation as the people of God languished and waited, ruled by darkness and evil. *(pause)* Finally, in the fullness of time, there was in the city of Nazareth, a virgin named Mary who was betrothed to Joseph. An angel of the Lord appeared to Mary and said, "Be not afraid! Rejoice, for the Lord has found favor in you. The Holy Spirit shall come upon you and you shall bear a son and His name shall be called Jesus." *(music begins)* Mary was at first afraid of the meaning of Gabriel's words. But then she answered, "Let it be to me according to your word. My soul magnifies the Lord and I am not afraid. Joseph was also visited by an angel of the Lord and heard the assurance that this was indeed God's plan. So he took Mary as his wife and held her in his heart. He too said, "I trust in the Lord and I am not afraid."

Do Not Be Afraid

Thus it was that when Mary was great with child, she and Joseph traveled to Bethlehem, to be counted in a census as ordered by the Roman Emperor. While there, Mary gave birth to a Son, wrapped Him in swaddling clothes, and laid Him in a manger, as there was no room for them at the inn. It became clear to all who saw Him that this tiny sleeping Child was the Son of God, the Savior, the promised King. This Child was God's messenger of love, peace and hope to the cold and silent earth. There, in the humblest of places, surrounded by simple shepherds and lowly creatures, Mary took the baby Jesus in her tender arms and whispered, "A miracle is born this holy night. A miracle is born this holy night."

A Miracle This Holy Night

And so it had come to pass that on this holiest of nights, this night of miracles, Christ the Savior was born! The heavens rang with angelic sounds and the light of the power and glory of God shone all around. The angels sang, "Glory to God in the highest and on earth, peace and goodwill to all! Christ is born! Christ is born, sing glory to God!"

Christ Is Born, Sing Glory to God!

Word of Jesus' birth quickly spread and the people praised God for all that was told to them. Angels had brought good tidings of great joy to those waiting in darkness. Those who had persevered with faith in their hearts and believed in the promise were touched by God's gracious love. People everywhere fell to their knees, praising God and saying, "I have heard His word and I trust in the Lord. I have heard the truth. I have been touched by God and I believe."

I Was Touched and I Believe

(music begins) It all began that single miraculous holy night, over two thousand years ago, in the little town of Bethlehem. It began with a promise – a promise made to a people that one day they would be saved. Instead of being saved by a fierce warrior leading a strong army, they – and we – were saved by a tiny Child; a Child of miracles, a Child of everlasting light. Through faith in Jesus, our fears are placed upon His shoulders and He grants us His peace. Through faith in Him, He takes away our sins and gives us His love. This Child is God's promise fulfilled. Through faith in Him, we receive one of God's greatest miracles: the gift of hope.

Child of Hope

This day we celebrate that first holy night of miracles. We give thanks to God for sending His only Son to earth to save us. Let us rededicate ourselves to the God of hope and, like shepherds on that first Christmas night, let us renew our commitment to tell the world of the miracle of Jesus' birth. Christ was born to save us. His message is still one of hope and love. Rejoice and tell the world that the miracle lives on. Christ has come for all! Come. Let us worship Christ, the newborn King!

Worship Christ, the Newborn King!